MW01537761

100 WRITING PROMPTS

Let Your Imagination Run Wild!

NOVEMBER 12, 2018

WRITTEN BY MICKEY CRABTREE
www.mickey-crabtree.com

ISBN: 9781731226501

This writing journal belongs to:

Read this first!

How to use this book:

First, grab a notebook, notepad or a stack of papers and a pencil!

Second, read the writing prompt at the top of the page!

Third, let your imagination run wild!

Use the space below the prompt to write a story or doodle some ideas. The extra paper you grabbed is incase you run out of room to write!

Pro tip: Write your stories in a notebook so you can re-use this writing prompt book. Save all your stories and compare them over time!

Write a short story about what it would be like to have a pet dinosaur!

Imagine if you were a GIANT! What would you do?

You go to the zoo and can understand all the animals. What are they saying?

Write a story with these words: banana, airplane, hippo, xylophone, wood.

You discovered a new planet. Describe the planet. What did you name it and why?

Write about your favorite place. What do you like the most about it?

You wake up in a bird's nest. How did you get there? How will you get out?

What is your favorite holiday? Why?

If you could have one wish come true, what would it be?

A witch put a spell on you! What type of spell was cast? How will you break it?

Is there something you are good at doing?
Write about it!

You are the captain of a pirate ship... that can fly! Write about your day.

Describe what you look like.

You build a snowman and it comes to life!
What do you do next?

What are you afraid of? Why?

Imagine you find an alien spaceship in your backyard. What does it look like? What do the aliens look like? Why are they in your backyard?

Write a short story with these 3 words:
mop, lasagna, artist.

Describe your favorite TV character.

Would you rather have a pet cat or tiger? Why?

Describe a world where everything is the same color.

You live on a farm, but not any farm. A farm with WACKY animals no one has ever heard of before! What types of animals are they and what are they called?

What is your favorite game? Describe it.

ALL shoes have disappeared! Describe how it feels to walk barefoot everywhere.

Follow a rainbow to where it ends. What is waiting there?

Describe where you live.

Create a video game. What is it called? How do you play?

There's a crash in your living room! Your cat has turned into a unicorn! What happens next?

Create 5 knock-knock jokes.

You find a skeleton key and an old map on your bed. Where does the map lead you? What does the key open?

Invent a new word. How do you spell it? What does it mean? Use it in a sentence.

Write about your favorite food. Why is it your favorite?

You find a time machine! Where in time do you go? Why? What do you find?

How can you help make the world a better place?

Describe your eyes. Get a mirror and look closely. Are they one solid color? Are there specks of different colors?

Write an action story with the words: fire, princess, watermelon, lizard, French horn.

Why does the Tooth Fairy collect teeth?

You are on the beach. Describe what you see, hear, feel and smell.

You are given a note that says, "You will turn into a fish tomorrow." What happens next?

You find a magic lamp. Is there a genie inside?

A package full of mechanical parts arrives for you. What do you build and why?

Describe what you see when you look through a telescope.

If you can have any superpower, what would it be? Why? How will you use it?

Something pulled your fishing rod into the water! What was it?

Write about climbing a mountain. Why are you climbing it? What do you see? What is at the top?

A BIG thunderstorm is rolling in. What does it look like? What does is sound like? How does it make you feel?

Write a letter to a friend. Tell them why you like being their friend.

There is a gorilla loose and it is your job to take it back to the zoo! How do you do that?

There are fairies living in the flower bed by your front door. Why are they living there?

Would you rather go scuba diving or ride in a hot air balloon? Why?

You are a prince or princess. How do you spend your day?

Write about your favorite memory.

How does a tree feel when it loses its leaves?

Create a superhero! What is their super power? What are they called? Why are they a superhero?

You find a very lucky penny on the sidewalk. Who do you give the lucky penny to? Why?

Why do clouds float?

Write a fairy tale about a mighty wizard that awakens a fire-breathing dragon!

What is your favorite book or story? Why?

Describe how music makes you feel.

If you could do ***anything*** right now, what would you do?

Create a villain! What do they look like? What is their name? Why are they bad?

Think about a vegetable you do not like.
Write a letter to that vegetable explaining why you don't like it.

A volcano is about to erupt! How does the volcano feel? Nervous, excited, scared?

Would you rather play hide-and-seek or tag? Why?

Your family gets you a robot. What does the robot do?

Write about your favorite family tradition.

What do birds talk about when they migrate?

Does a toothbrush like being a toothbrush?
Why or why not?

Write a poem that rhymes including these words: house, cows, eyebrows.

There is a new teacher in your classroom. What happened to your old teacher?

What do you want to be when you grow up? Why?

How does a butterfly feel when they fly for the first time?

Rewrite a classic story: The 3 little pigs are bullies and the wolf is very nice.

What is your favorite thing? Describe it.

A squirrel needs your help! Why?

Pretend your pet goldfish can talk. What do they like to talk about?

How can you help a neighbor?

A monster is afraid of the dark. Write them a letter to make them feel better.

What is something you want to be better at? Write about it.

What do bears dream about when they hibernate?

Write a song!

Imagine if EVERYTHING glows in the dark at night. What does it look like at night?

Write a short story about a small pig that likes to swim in the ocean.

If you could change your name, what would you change it to? Why?

Pretend your refrigerator is a portal to another world! Where does it take you?

If the Moon is made of cheese, what is the Sun made of?

You are a collector! What do you collect and why? Where do you find the items?

Write a funny ghost story.

You win the school spelling bee! What was the winning word? How did it feel to win?

Write a mysterious note to a brave scientist who has a jetpack.

You have a pet giraffe. What do you do for fun together?

What do you think about when you lay down to go to sleep?

Describe how a snowflake feels knowing they are different from every other snowflake.

Describe the favorite dessert of a crazy space monster who sees in the dark.

You visit a fortune teller. What do they see in the crystal ball?

The entire town is frozen! How do you save the day?

Describe what flowers smell like.

Invent the first flying car! What does it look like? How does it fly?

If you were a spider, what designs would you weave in your web?

Compare an orange and a golf ball. How are they similar? How are they different?

The Pharaoh wants you to build a pyramid! How will you build it? What will it look like?

ABOUT THE AUTHOR!

MICKEY CRABTREE IS A DAYDREAMER. THE WRITING PROMPTS IN THIS BOOK ARE SOME OF THE THINGS SHE THINKS ABOUT DURING THE DAY! SHE *REALLY* DOES WONDER WHAT BEARS DREAM ABOUT WHILE THEY HIBERNATE!

MICKEY CRABTREE IS PROUD TO BE A CHILDREN'S BOOK AND MIDDLE GRADE AUTHOR AND ILLUSTRATOR. SHE HOPES THIS BOOK HELPS ENCOURAGE YOU TO FOLLOW YOUR DREAMS AND WRITE CREATIVE STORIES.

LET YOUR IDEAS RUN WILD!

Made in the USA
Coppell, TX
10 December 2019

12692037R00120